Old MacDonald Had a Farm

For Joanna

DUTTON

Published by the Penguin Group
Penguin Books Ltd, 27 Wrights Lane, London W8 5TZ, England
Penguin Books USA Inc., 375 Hudson Street, New York, New York 10014, USA
Penguin Books Australia Ltd, Ringwood, Victoria, Australia
Penguin Books Canada Ltd, 10 Alcorn Avenue, Toronto, Ontario, Canada M4V 3B2
Penguin Books (NZ) Ltd, 182–190 Wairau Road, Auckland 10, New Zealand

Penguin Books Ltd, Registered Offices: Harmondsworth, Middlesex, England

First published in 1991 by Blackie
This edition first published 1992
Reissued in Dutton 1995
10 9 8 7 6 5 4 3 2 1

Printed in Hong Kong by Wing King Tong Co. Ltd

A CIP catalogue record for this book is available from the British Library

Old MacDonald Had a Farm

The Traditional Nursery Song

Illustrated by
Prue Theobalds

DUTTON

Old MacDonald had a farm, E–I–E–I–O!
And on that farm he had some sheep, E–I–E–I–O!
With a baa, baa here and a baa, baa there,
Here a baa, there a baa, everywhere a baa, baa,
Old MacDonald had a farm, E–I–E–I–O!

Old MacDonald had a farm, E–I–E–I–O!
And on that farm he had some dogs, E–I–E–I–O!
With a woof, woof here and a woof, woof there,
Here a woof, there a woof, everywhere a woof, woof,
Old MacDonald had a farm, E–I–E–I–O!

Old MacDonald had a farm,
  E–I–E–I–O!
And on that farm he had a horse,
  E–I–E–I–O!
With a neigh, neigh here
And a neigh, neigh there,
Here a neigh, there a neigh,
Everywhere a neigh, neigh,
Old MacDonald had a farm,
  E–I–E–I–O!

Old MacDonald had a farm, E–I–E–I–O!
And on that farm he had some geese, E–I–E–I–O!
With a honk, honk here and a honk, honk there,
Here a honk, there a honk, everywhere a honk, honk,
Old MacDonald had a farm E–I–E–I–O!

Old MacDonald had a farm, E–I–E–I–O!
And on that farm he had some cows, E–I–E–I–O!
With a moo, moo here and a moo, moo there,
Here a moo, there a moo, everywhere a moo, moo,
Old MacDonald had a farm, E–I–E–I–O!

Old MacDonald had a farm, E–I–E–I–O!
And on that farm he had some chickens, E–I–E–I–O!
With a cluck, cluck here and a cluck, cluck there,
Here a cluck, there a cluck, everywhere a cluck, cluck,
Old MacDonald had a farm, E–I–E–I–O!

Old MacDonald had a farm, E–I–E–I–O!
And on that farm he had some ducks, E–I–E–I–O!
With a quack, quack here and a quack, quack there,
Here a quack, there a quack, everywhere a quack, quack,
Old MacDonald had a farm, E–I–E–I–O!

Old MacDonald had a farm, E–I–E–I–O!
And on that farm he had some goats, E–I–E–I–O!
With a meh, meh here and a meh, meh there,
Here a meh, there a meh, everywhere a meh, meh,
Old MacDonald had a farm, E–I–E–I–O!

Old MacDonald had a farm, E–I–E–I–O!
And on that farm he had some pigs, E–I–E–I–O!
With an oink, oink here and an oink, oink there,
Here an oink, there an oink, everywhere an oink, oink,
Old MacDonald had a farm, E–I–E–I–O!

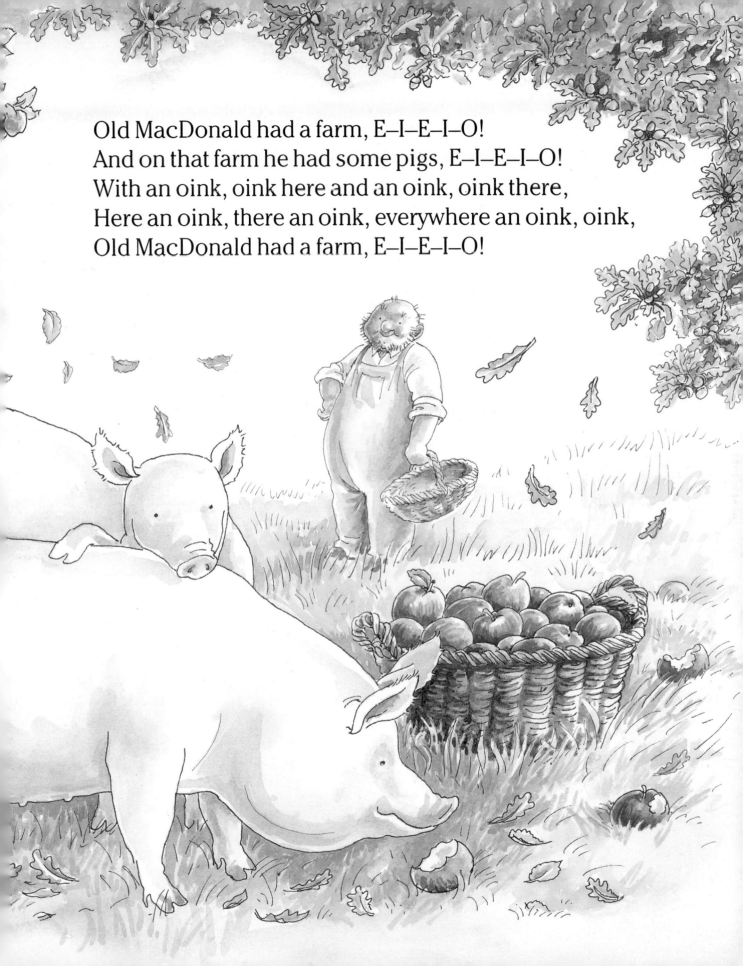

Old MacDonald had a farm, E–I–E–I–O!
And on that farm he had some cats, E–I–E–I–O!
With a miaow, miaow here and a miaow, miaow there,
Here a miaow, there a miaow,
  everywhere a miaow, miaow,
Old MacDonald had a farm, E–I–E–I–O!

Old MacDonald had a farm, E–I–E–I–O!
And on that farm he had some turkeys, E–I–E–I–O!
With a gobble, gobble here and a gobble, gobble there,
Here a gobble, there a gobble, everywhere a gobble, gobble,
Old MacDonald had a farm, E–I–E–I–O!

Old MacDonald had a farm, E–I–E–I–O!
And on that farm he had a donkey, E–I–E–I–O!

With a hee-haw here and a hee-haw there,
Here a hee, there a haw, everywhere a hee-haw,
Old MacDonald had a farm, E–I–E–I–O!